Tortoise and Hare

Story written by Cynthia Rider
Illustrated by Tim Archbold

Speed Sounds

Consonants

Ask children to say the sounds.

f	l	m	n	r	s	v	z	**sh**	**th**	**ng**
ff	ll	mm	nn	**rr**	ss	ve	zz			**nk**
	le		kn		**se**		se			
					ce		s			

b	c	d	g	h	j	p	qu	t	w	x	y	**ch**
bb	k	dd	gg			pp		tt	**wh**			tch
	ck											

Each box contains one sound but sometimes more than one grapheme.
*Focus graphemes for this story are **circled**.*

Vowels

Ask children to say the sounds in and out of order.

a	e ea	i	o	u	ay	ee y	igh	ow
at	hen	in	on	up	day	see	high	blow

oo	oo	ar	or	air	ir	ou	oy
zoo	look	car	for	fair	whirl	shout	boy

Story Green Words

Ask children to read the words first in Fred Talk and then say the word.

crow dash rush hop skip plod sheep grow plod

Ask children to say the syllables and then read the whole word.

hurr|y a|way sparr|ow ver|y

Ask children to read the root first and then the whole word with the suffix.

slow → slowly gasp → gasps speed → speeds cheep → cheeps bellow → bellows

Red Words

Ask children to practise reading the words across the rows, down the columns and in and out of order clearly and quickly.

I'm	you	he	tortoise*
hare*	race*	the	want
I've	they	onto	what
of	are	she	I'll

* Red Word in this book only

Tortoise and Hare

Introduction

Have you ever seen a tortoise and a hare? Tortoises move really slowly, carrying their shells on their backs while hares hop around quickly.

In this story Hare asks Tortoise to have a race to show that he's the fastest. Off they go, with Hare speeding away and Tortoise plodding along slowly. It seems that Hare is going to win easily, until he does something rather silly. Let's find out what he does.

Tortoise is plodding slowly along when Hare runs up.

"Hurry up, sleepy," says Hare.

"I'm not as slow as you think,"

says Tortoise.

"Let's have a race, then," says Hare.

"A race!" gasps Tortoise.

"Yes," says Hare.

"1 ... 2 ... 3 ... Run!" says Crow.

Hare speeds away ...
dash, rush, hop, skip.

Tortoise follows ... plod, plod, plod.

"Hurry!" bellows a sheep.

"Hurry!" cheeps a sparrow.

Hare sees that Tortoise is a long way back.

He sits and rests.

He grows very sleepy ...

Zzz! Zzz!

Tortoise plods slowly past Hare.

On and on he plods.

On and on ... and ...

... Tortoise wins the race!

Questions to talk about

Ask children to TTYP for each question using 'Fastest finger' (FF) or 'Have a think' (HaT).

p.8	(FF)	What is Tortoise doing when Hare runs up?
p.9	(HaT)	What does Tortoise think of the idea of having a race?
p.10	(HaT)	How is Hare at the start of the race?
	(HaT)	Who do you think the sheep and the sparrow want to win?
p.11	(FF)	What does Hare do when he sees that Tortoise is a long way behind?
pp.12–13	(HaT)	Why does Tortoise win the race?